I0901298

Marion Gabrielle

The Weekender

HONG KONG

COLLECTIVE SHORTS
by NHP PUBLISHING

If someone had told me that one day, I would live in Hong Kong, chances are I wouldn't have believed it. People and media often paint Hong Kong as this fast-paced, business-oriented city (and also something of a party hub), whereas I enjoy a slower pace of life, punctuated with cultural and artistic experiences. Yet in 2024, I found myself, my belongings and my cameras, on a long flight to Hong Kong.

From the start, I was inspired by Hong Kong's undeniable cool vibe, by its colours, architecture, busy street life and mix of cultures. And through photography, I met people who are passionate visual storytellers, capturing and recapturing their city through different angles and investing in its rich cultural life.

For travellers, Hong Kong has all the advantages of big metropolises, minus some of their frustrations. With a reasonable size and great transport links, it is easy to navigate, and safe to explore. In one day, you could easily go for a hike with breathtaking views, have lunch at a cosy café, visit a temple or museum, indulge in some shopping, and end the day with live music and world renown cocktails. For those who prefer a relaxed experience, hop on a ferry for an island day trip to enjoy beaches, views, and seafood.

The Weekender – Hong Kong is a visual invitation to a long weekend in the city, taking you along to some of my favourite spots throughout Hong Kong Island and Kowloon. Of course, this book encapsulates my own experience as a Westerner living in Hong Kong part-time, albeit mediated and enriched by a partner who was born there (and has a great moustache). As such, it has, I hope, both an outsider and an insider perspective.

All the images in this book were shot on film, as analogue photography is a significant part of my work. Not only does film capture light beautifully, but shooting analogue invites the photographer to reflect on their practice, to consider each shot, to slow down and observe. Part of the fun also lies in the unexpected results you sometimes get when developing your rolls! Photographing this book on film was a pleasure and a real challenge, and I have learned a lot in the process, which I'll take with me on my next adventure.

Marion Gabrielle

TAXI
TAXI 4 SEATS

Thursday

Hong Kong, SAR

Thursday 6 PM

香港站
Hong Kong Station

M+
Kennedy Town

Thursday 6:28 PM

Check-in at The Fleming Hotel, Wan Chai

Thursday 7:35 PM

Drinks at Osteria Marzia

Looking for the last neons signs Thursday 9 PM

東方小祗園齋菜

Thursday 10:30 PM

Wrapping up the day

GC 400 KODAK
10
KODAK GC 400
11
GC 400 KODAK

TAXI
機械防水公司
誠興
麻雀公司
16
17

Friday

Waking up at The Fleming

Friday 7:15 AM

RETRO
Breakfast set
Beverage +
Morning toast
Lunch set
Tea set
Pancake
1666

Friday 8:04 AM

Breakfast at Retro

Crossing the bay on the Star Ferry Friday 9:25 AM

THE STAR FERRY CO. LTD
484P.
星 MERIDIAN
10
9

中国建设银行

Friday 10:10 AM Soaking up contemporary visual culture at M+ Museum

東展廳
East Galleries

A Walk in Kowloon Park

Friday 2 PM

Friday 3:05 PM Yau Ma Tei Temple

勝利麻雀
娛樂
冠南華
Koon Nam

Friday 4:15 PM

Fa Yuen Street Market, Mong Kok

A stop by the film shop, Tsim Sha Tsui

Friday 6 PM

Billy, owner of T5SWF

Friday 9 PM Hong Kong siu mai and curry fish balls, Temple Street Market

41
KODAK 200
42
KODAK 200
43
KODAK

9
9A
10
10A
11
11A
12

Saturday

Saturday 8:25 AM

Hiking the Dragon's Back trail

Dimsum
All Day

THE REMATCH
ROCKY
BALBOA
APOLLO
CREED
ROCKY II
TICKETS ON SALE AT BOXOFFICE
EMPIRE
STRIKES BACK
帝國反擊戰
SEIKO
飲屈臣
贏到哈哈笑

PEPSI

Saturday 12 PM

Dim sum at Lang's Café

洪聖古廟

泰利
TAXI
TAXI
KC
429

MONOCLE ALPINE
BODY LOTION
MONOCLE ALPINE
BODY SOAP
Bangkok
Bangkok
MUSGO REAL
St.Moritz
St.Moritz

Saturday 3 PM

MONOCLE, Wan Chai

MONOCLE
Scent Two: Laurel
Eau de Toilette
MONOCLE
News/Books/Stationery/Travel Musts

A ride on the iconic Ding Ding, Causeway Bay

Saturday 3:45 PM

麻辣派對
CHILI PARTY
deliveroo 戶戶送
惠無花假!
外賣自取
全單
半價
5649 6988
deliveroo 戶戶送
IKEA

門口土地

Saturday 7:10 PM

Thai curry and pandan ice cream at Samsen

Saturday 9 PM After dinner cocktails at The Savory Project

Sunday

MTR Central Station

Sunday 9:45 AM

TON
TAXI

的士
TAXI

買三送一杯
$33
ORDER HERE 在此下單
DRINKS MENU
HOT FOOD MENU
STEP 1
PICK YOUR DRINK
養生
THE NORTH FACE
打卡
$19
$29
SHOP225

Going up the Central escalator

Sunday 11:04 AM

LUSH
SPA

精美小食
蘭芳園
AN FONG YULN

PEANUTS

Sunday 12:45 PM

Sheung Wan

蓮香

68
20

Sunday 1:05 PM Lunch, coffee and a curated playlist at Rootdown

聖宮
千祥百福蔭羣生
列聖諸神崇一體

Sunday 2:35 PM Man Mo Temple

王
閻

Afternoon treats at Goose Chocolate

Sunday 4:15 PM

開運

GOOSE'CHOCOLATE

STAUNTO
A
BLOCK

Sunday 5:20 PM PMQ, Central

STORE

A ride to Victoria Peak to see the sunset

Sunday 6:20 PM

Sunday 8:15 PM

Departure from Hong Kong International Airport Sunday 9 PM

The Weekender

HONG KONG

Published by New Heroes & Pioneers
Photography and text: Marion Gabrielle
Creative Direction: Francois Le Bled
Series Book Design: Daniel Zachrisson
Edition Book Design: Lilith Onyett
Model: Francis Kwong

Print and bound by BALTO print (Lithuania)
Legal deposit December 2024
ISBN 9789198656596

MIX
Paper | Supporting responsible forestry
FSC® C107574

Copyright 2024 New Heroes & Pioneers. All rights reserved.
Reproduction in whole or in part is prohibited without the authorisation of the publisher and the photographer.

"Many thanks to Francis for his patience with posing and his help with translating; to Anna for her unfaltering support; to Billy for taking good care of my film images; and to Francois for making this book possible."
Marion Gabrielle

The Fleming Hotel - thefleming.com
Osteria Mazria - osteriamarzia.com.hk
Retro - instagram.com/cafe.retro.hk
M+ Museum - mplus.org.hk
Time Fly Slow With Film - timeflyslowithfilm.com
Lang's Café - instagram.com/langs_cafe
The Monocle - monocle.com
Samsen - samsen-hk.com
The Savory Project - thesavoryproject.com
Central Market - centralmarket.hk
Rootdown Café - instagram.com/rootdown.hk
Man Mo Temple - tungwah.org.hk (man-mo-temple)
Goose Chocolate - instagram.com/goose_chocolate
PMQ - pmq.org.hk

COLLECTIVE SHORTS
by NHP PUBLISHING